KU-242-233

*V*isiting the *P*ast

The D-Day Landing Sites

940.54

Stockton Borough Public Libraries 3|03

0041934601

B o b   R e e s

Heinemann
LIBRARY

www.heinemann.co.uk/library

Visit our website to find out more information about Heinemann Library books.

To order:

☎ Phone 44 (0) 1865 888066

🖹 Send a fax to 44 (0) 1865 314091

🖥 Visit the Heinemann Bookshop at www.heinemann.co.uk/library to browse our catalogue and order online.

First published in Great Britain by Heinemann Library, Halley Court, Jordan Hill, Oxford OX2 8EJ, a division of Reed Educational and Professional Publishing Ltd. Heinemann is a registered trademark of Reed Educational & Professional Publishing Ltd.

OXFORD MELBOURNE AUCKLAND JOHANNESBURG BLANTYRE
GABORONE IBADAN PORTSMOUTH NH (USA) CHICAGO

© Reed Educational and Professional Publishing Ltd 2002
The moral right of the proprietor has been asserted.

All rights reserved. No part of this publication may be reproduced, stored in a retrieval system, or transmitted in any form or by any means, electronic, mechanical, photocopying, recording, or otherwise without either the prior written permission of the Publishers or a licence permitting restricted copying in the United Kingdom issued by the Copyright Licensing Agency Ltd, 90 Tottenham Court Road, London W1P OLP.

Designed by Visual Image
Illustrations by Paul Bale
Originated by Ambassador Litho Ltd
Printed by Wing King Tong in Hong Kong/China

ISBN 0 431 02787 0
06 05 04 03 02
10 9 8 7 6 5 4 3 2 1

British Library Cataloguing in Publication Data

Rees, Bob
The D-Day landing sites. – (Visiting the past)
1. World War, 1939–45 – Campaigns – France – Normandy – Juvenile literature
I. Title
940.5'4'2142

Acknowledgements

To every man and woman who gave so much, even their lives, so that we can enjoy today.

The publishers would like to thank Martin Sookias for permission to reproduce all photographs with the exception of the following: Corbis: p.20 (right); Hulton Getty: p.18; Imperial War Museum: p.5.

Cover photograph reproduced with permission of Corbis.

Every effort has been made to contact copyright holders of any material reproduced in this book. Any omissions will be rectified in subsequent printings if notice is given to the Publishers.

Any words appearing in the text in bold, **like this**, are explained in the Glossary.

Contents

The D-Day landings — why?

The beach you can see in this photograph has been a favourite for seaside holidays for over a hundred years. Yet on 6 June 1944, this beach and others like it that stretch for about 50 miles along the Normandy coastline were the scene of bloody fighting. Thousands of soldiers from Britain, Canada and the USA landed from the sea to attack the German army. Why did this happen?

This is the beach at Hermanville-sur-Mer. It was part of Sword beach where British soldiers landed on D-Day. The shallow, sandy beach was ideal for **landing craft** to unload soldiers and equipment. Today it has returned to being a family holiday location.

In 1944, the war against **Nazi** Germany, which was part of the Second World War, had lasted for nearly five years. The **Allies**, particularly Britain and the USA had realized that they needed to invade Western Europe if they were going to defeat **Hitler** and Nazi Germany. In 1943, President Franklin D. Roosevelt of the USA and Winston Churchill, Prime Minister of the UK, had decided that there would be a landing in Normandy between May and June 1944. The landings would be named 'Overlord'. There were to be five landing beaches. At the western end the American forces would land at beaches called 'Utah' and 'Omaha'. British soldiers would land at 'Gold' and 'Sword' beaches and between them Canadian troops would land at 'Juno'. General Dwight D. Eisenhower was in charge as Supreme Commander. General Montgomery was Commander in Chief of the armies.

The amount of organization needed was amazing. Hundreds of thousands of soldiers needed to be gathered together and trained. Millions of tons of supplies and weapons needed to be produced. Ships had to be built to transport the soldiers. Even an artificial port was built to be towed to France to help land supplies.

It was highly important to have knowledge about the landing beaches and the German defences. The **French Resistance**, Allied secret agents in France, aerial photography and **frogmen** who swam ashore from submarines at night all provided this information. Secrecy was also vital. How could they keep such a big operation secret? The troops were kept isolated and couldn't speak to anyone. Lots of false information was given out. This was to persuade the Germans that the landings would be made near Calais, miles away from the real site. That way the German defenders were still not sure where the 'main' landings would be, even when the Allied soldiers were coming ashore in Normandy. 'D-Day' was simply the code name for the day of the landings. It has no other meaning.

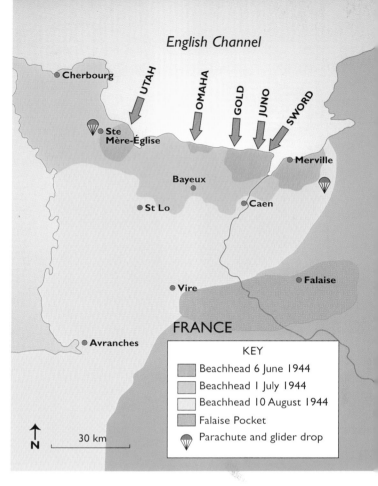

This map shows the beaches in northern France where the Allied armies landed on D-Day.

These men led Operation Overlord. Standing left to right: General Bradley in charge of US troops, Admiral Ramsay in charge of sea operations, Air Marshal Leigh-Mallory in charge of air operations, US General Bedell-Smith who was Chief of Staff. Sitting left to right: Air Chief Marshal Tedder Deputy Supreme Commander, General Eisenhower Supreme Commander, General Montgomery in charge of British and Canadian troops.

The Atlantic Wall

In January 1944, Field Marshal Rommel, hero of the German army fighting in Africa, was put in charge of defending the coast from Saint Nazaire in western France to Holland. This was part of the 'Atlantic Wall' built to protect German occupied Europe from attack by the **Allies**. The Wall was a series of concrete fortifications with guns and radar. Between these **strong-points** the defences were often much weaker. As early as 1942, the Germans had decided that landings were unlikely in Normandy because there were rocky reefs in places just offshore.

This large gun is one of four at the German 'Chaos' battery at Longues-sur-Mer. After heavy bombing, they were engaged by the **battleship** USS *Arkansas*, cruiser HMS *Ajax*, and the Free French cruisers *Georges-Leygues* and *Montcalm*. The warships finally silenced the German guns at 7 p.m. on D-Day.

The 'Wurzburg' German radar dish at Douvres-la-Déliverande was the only dish among five radars not destroyed by bombing. However, it did not spot the Allied fleet because the Allies had jammed its operations. The radar site was captured after eleven days of Allied attacks after D-Day.

At Ouistreham there was an artillery range-finding post that controlled the guns protecting the mouth of the River Orne. The soldiers serving there were completely self-contained. They even had their own air pumping system so that they could seal off the bunker and still operate if they were attacked. This is their living and sleeping quarters.

When Rommel took over he immediately decided that the Normandy section of the defences was too weak. Some sections were not finished. French workmen had slowed up building because they opposed the German occupation of France. There were not enough **mines** and some gun **batteries** didn't have the right guns. He ordered that more defences should be built. Fields were flooded and wooden or metal spikes were put in areas where planes and **gliders** were likely to land. The defences included **reinforced concrete bunkers** for big guns to fire out to sea from, radar stations to detect any Allied activity, **pill–boxes** and strong-points containing machine guns and **artillery**, and **command posts** to control the defences.

On the beaches there were anti–tank ditches, wire entanglements, metal spikes and concrete bocks all with explosive mines to stop **landing craft** and invading soldiers and tanks. The Atlantic Wall was a strong barrier. If Allied landings were to be successful, then **engineers** would have to break their way though the barriers, clear the mines and blow up the defences.

Stockton Borough Public Libraries

Weapons

The weapons used by the two competing forces were crucial to the outcome of the D-Day landings and following battles. Troops on both sides had the kind of personal weapons that soldiers had in all areas of fighting in the Second World War – rifles, grenades, machine guns and **mortars**. Both sides had tanks, **mines** and **artillery**.

The Germans had two advantages. Their 'Tiger' tanks had more powerful guns than the **Allied** tanks and thicker **armour**, so they were difficult to destroy. The German '88 mm' artillery anti-tank gun was highly destructive and could fire long distances. They destroyed hundreds of Allied tanks.

The Allies greatest advantage was that they would have *more* of everything. They would be able to afford to lose hundreds of tanks to the German '88s' because there would be hundreds more available at the supply depots. There were thousands of guns and millions of shells. American factories produced all this. The second advantage was that the Allies would control the air and the sea. By 1944, the **Luftwaffe** had been forced to concentrate on the defence of German towns against non-stop bombing raids by the Allies. German planes were also fighting the Russian advance from the East. German planes that were in the area would be overwhelmed by Allied planes, so the Allied planes could bomb and **strafe** without opposition in the air. Air power would play a big part in the final destruction of the German forces in Normandy. At sea, the German **U-boat** threat had been defeated in the **Battle of the Atlantic** so supplies of men and material could be brought safely from America. Allied supply routes to the landing

The armoury in the German range-finding post at Ouistreham shows the personal defence weapons and equipment used there. Rifles, sub machine-guns, ammunition holders and metal helmets would all be needed in the event of attack.

beaches were uninterrupted. The warships of the Allied fleet would be able to bombard the German defences. Naval gunfire proved to be the most accurate of the **bombardments**. They had also developed landing ships' firing rockets which saturated their targets with explosives. Lastly, the British army developed special tanks to help take the beaches. The soldiers called them 'funnies' because they looked unusual.

The 'DD' (Duplex Drive) Sherman tank was specially developed for the D-Day landings to give armoured support at the moment the soldiers landed on the beaches. The tank had a rubber and canvas screen which allowed it to float and two propellers to drive it through the sea. Once ashore the screen was folded and it operated as a normal tank. The tank in the photograph is one of those which sank off Omaha beach in the rough sea. It was salvaged by French divers and is on display with other items found on the seabed.

Artillery – big guns used to destroy enemy soldiers, tanks and equipment – was widely used in the fighting in Normandy. This is a British 5.5 inch (13.9 centimetre) gun on display at the Merville **battery**.

Pegasus bridge

The first place to be attacked by British soldiers during the night of 5 June was the bridge over the Caen canal at Bénouville. The aim was to stop German **reinforcements** from Caen reaching the British landings at Sword Beach. The specially trained **assault troops**, led by Major John Howard, were to land in **gliders** and capture the bridge. They were part of the airborne landings of the 6th Airborne Division trying to protect the eastern end of the D-Day landings. The pilots of the first three gliders were able to land their aircraft in the marshy ground right next to the bridge.

After fighting briefly, Howard's men captured the bridge and made sure that the Germans had left no explosives to blow it up. Their job now was to hold it against German **counter-attack** until troops arrived from Sword Beach. All night the Germans tried to recapture the bridge using tanks and even gun-boats on the river, but they did not succeed. Eventually Lord Lovat's Brigade of **commandos** arrived to relieve Major Howard's men. The first objective of D-Day was a total success. The bridge was renamed 'Pegasus' after the winged horse which was the badge of the British airborne division.

The capture of the bridge at Bénouville was important to the success of the plans for D-Day. The original Pegasus bridge was worn out by the 1990s. After many arguments over what should happen the bridge was removed and is on display at the Pegasus bridge museum, to the east of the new bridge. A new bridge, shown here, was opened in May 1994, just in time for the 50th anniversary celebrations of the D-Day landings.

The Merville battery

A battery of four massive concrete bunkers containing big guns at Merville, just east of Pegasus bridge, was also a target. The guns were defended by machine guns, wire and mines. There was a plan to demolish the guns, which involved heavy bombing followed by a landing of 750 paratroops. It all went wrong. The bombers missed the target. The wind and the defences caused the parachutists to be scattered over a wide area. When Colonel Otway, the leader of the 9th Battalion Parachute Regiment, landed he could only gather 150 men and no heavy weapons or equipment. He decided to attack anyway, yelling to his troops 'Get in, get in', and in desperate hand to hand fighting the battery was captured and the guns silenced. Of the 130 defenders of Merville only 22 were left alive or not seriously wounded. Of the 150 attackers only about 75 could walk away. It was later said, 'They didn't know it was impossible, they just did it.'

This is one of the four heavily defended, re-inforced concrete **artillery** blockhouses of the Merville battery that were captured by the men of the 9th Parachute Battalion. The guns were later re-occupied by the Germans and then re-captured by British commandos. Most importantly, the guns were unable to fire during the vital landing times at Sword beach.

British soldiers who had captured Pegasus bridge knocked on the door of the Café Gondrée. It was the first house to be liberated in France on D-Day. When Monsieur Gondrée realized he had been liberated he dug up some bottles of champagne he had hidden in the garden and gave them to the troops. The café is the scene of annual reunions by veterans of the action there.

11

Sainte Mère-Église

The **Allies** needed to capture the port of Cherbourg as quickly as possible. The plan was to parachute American troops into the area around a little town called Sainte Mère-Église and join up with the soldiers landing at Utah Beach. They would cut off the road to Cherbourg so that no German **reinforcements** could get through to help the port.

The bad weather on the night of 5 June meant that many of the parachutists went off course. Some were drowned in the low-lying fields that had been flooded on Rommel's orders. Most units were broken up and could not find their way to where they were supposed to be. The American troops had been issued with tin toys called 'crickets' which made a clicking noise. These were supposed to help them recognize each other in the dark. Some of these were captured by German soldiers who realized what they were for and used the crickets to lure American soldiers into ambushes. All this confusion actually helped the Allies because it spread the fighting over a wide area, so the German generals had to spread their forces to the north and west rather than concentrate them where the seaborne landings would take place.

The ordeal of John Steele is still commemorated in Sainte Mère-Église. A model paratrooper is suspended from the church tower by a parachute. An inn is also named after him in the village.

Brigadier-General James 'Jumping Jim' Gavin of the US 82nd Airborne Division led the remnants of his troops in defence against German **counter-attacks** in the Sainte Mère-Église area.

Many of the US Airborne troops parachuted from Douglas C-47 'Skytrain' aircraft. They are better known by their British name 'Dakota'. This plane was in action during D-Day. It is now preserved in the Airborne museum at Sainte Mère-Église.

The 82nd Division of the Airborne forces landed around Sainte Mère-Église. Some landed in the town by mistake and were killed by the German **garrison**. One parachutist, John Steele, had the bad luck to have his parachute catch on the church tower in the town square. He struggled to get free but was noticed by a German soldier who fired at him. He was hit in the foot. He decided to '**play dead**' and had to hang on the tower until he was finally cut down by German troops and taken prisoner. The town was captured by American paratroops at around 5 a.m.

By dawn on D-Day the American Airborne forces had achieved their major goal of blocking the road to Cherbourg. Then they were able to assist in holding the **bridgehead** made by the troops that had landed on Utah Beach.

Memories of Joe Bressler, a US paratrooper

Bressler records the difficulties encountered in mass parachute landings at night: 'As I stepped forward I could hear a squish sound coming from my boot and felt warm blood. I had a really hard time walking. So I figured the German had hit me. Along came another trooper. I told him I couldn't walk and he told me to stay put and he would try to round up a few men. I waited about a half an hour and heard the "click-clock" – the distinctive noise of a toy cricket, our signaling device. At this point I met my close friend Prasse and he said "come on, lean on your rifle and try to walk forward." I limped along and made it into a large group of paratroopers where a medic examined my foot and determined that I had a compound fracture.'

'Fractured', from *Drop Zone Virtual Museum*'s Oral and E-histories.

The beaches: Omaha and Utah

From 4 a.m. on 6 June, **Allied** aircraft rained bombs down on the German defences along the Normandy coast. After that, the warships of the invasion fleet began to pound the defences with their heavy guns. The landings on the American beaches called 'Utah' and 'Omaha' began at 6.30 a.m. At Utah Beach, the American soldiers landed 2 kilometres south of the intended beach because of the strong currents. This turned out to be the weakest part of the whole coast. The low quality German troops there were bewildered by the sight of the Sherman DD tanks coming out of the sea and firing at them. Only 197 US soldiers were killed and wounded out of 23,000 who landed. The US 4th Division moved inland and met up with the US Airborne parachutists, dropped overnight, at Sainte Marie du Mont. The Americans met with tougher

There was a large **gun emplacement** on the Pointe du Hoc headland that could cause terrible damage at both Utah and Omaha Beach. It had been heavily bombed. The craters are still there today. US Rangers (**commandos**) scaled the cliffs. After a fierce fight the Rangers finally captured the gun placements. The Germans had already moved the guns.

Utah beach, today, is home to a museum that tells the story of events in 1944. There are many remnants of the landings on display around the site – landing craft, beach obstacles, guns, blockhouses, tanks and memorials.

fighting as they headed north, but their objective of cutting the road to Cherbourg was achieved.

The situation was worse on Omaha Beach. The bombers had missed their targets. The strong German defences had been reinforced without the Allies knowing. The sea was very rough. One DD tank battalion launched far out to sea. Only 2 out of 29 tanks reached the beach. The **landing craft** were caught by **artillery** and **automatic gunfire**. Forty per cent of the **engineers** who had to get rid of the beach obstacles were killed or wounded as they went into action. The American soldiers were trapped in a hail of German fire. However, just after midday, US engineers, spurred on by General Norman Cota, were able to make gaps in the sea wall and **barbed wire**. The German troops were running out of ammunition and Allied planes made sure that they could get no supplies. Eventually the Germans had to leave their positions. 'Bloody' Omaha Beach had been gained but at the cost of well over two thousand **casualties**.

Eyewitness

'We began to have casualties from small arms fire on the front deck, and as I backed away from the fire, I heard a blast and saw that a man wearing a flamethrower had been hit and the fuel tank was on fire. Several men standing nearby had burns. I noticed one man had a blister on his face that seemed to be six inches across. The man with the flamethrower was screaming in agony as he ran over to the starboard side and dived into the sea. I could see that even the soles of his boots were on fire. Here I was on Omaha Beach. Instead of being a fierce, well-trained, fighting infantryman, I was an exhausted, almost helpless, unarmed survivor of a shipwreck.'

Robert Walker, Omaha Beach,
116th Infantry Regiment,
US 29th Division

IN 1944

An American landing craft preserved at Utah beach. Vessels like these ferried the soldiers from the transport ships anchored offshore and carried them to the beach where the front ramp was lowered and the troops stormed up the beach.

15

Gold, Sword and Juno

At about 7.30 a.m., British and Canadian troops landed on the beaches codenamed 'Sword', 'Juno' and 'Gold'. Despite the fact that the **bombardment** had not destroyed many of the German defences, the landings started according to plan. **Engineers** began to get rid of the defences in the water. The specialised tanks beat pathways clear of **mines** on the beaches and began to destroy **pill-boxes**.

On Sword Beach the troops started to move inland. Soldiers of the 3rd Infantry Division and 51st Highland Brigade, supported by tanks and guns, headed south to Caen. The Germans resisted and prevented the capture of Caen. It was to take another month of bloody fighting to take the city.

Canadian losses at Juno Beach were heavier. The landing was delayed and **landing craft** became entangled in the beach defences as the tide rose. Despite severe losses the assault continued and the towns of Courseulles, Saint Aubin and Bernières were captured. The Canadian 3rd Division was able to link up with the British soldiers from Gold Beach but couldn't capture the airfield at Carpiquet near Caen or the main road nearby.

The British 50th (Northumberland) Division landed on Gold Beach. By 11 a.m., they had opened seven routes inland. The British troops linked up with the Canadians from Juno. They had also occupied the hills overlooking Arromanches, where the main supply port was to be built, and Port-en-Bessin, where fuel was to come ashore. At the end of D-Day the British and Canadian beaches had successfully achieved many of their **planned objectives** – but not all.

On Sword beach today holidaymakers have replaced soldiers. The damage has been repaired, but memorials to the people and events of D-Day remain.

This is a destroyed German reinforced concrete **gun emplacement** on the beach at Courseulles, Juno beach. Above the opening you can see the impact mark where a heavy shell, probably fired by an **Allied** warship, has struck the building.

Eyewitness

Bob Rees, the author's father, was an engineer on a landing ship. Here he remembers Gold Beach on D-Day: 'When we hit the beach the soldiers were glad to get off. They had been on board, in the Channel, in rough weather for several days. One of the sailors went ashore to hold a rope to help the soldiers ashore. He disappeared. He turned up later. He had followed the soldiers to see what it was like. There's no accounting for taste! Next morning a shipmate said "Did you hear that row as the **battleships** were firing all night?" I didn't. I was fast asleep I was so tired. As we left we passed HMS *Belfast* which was bombarding the shore. I got our **signaler** to send a message to my brother, Ernie, who was on board. The *Belfast* sent his greetings back!'

This **AVRE** (Armoured Vehicle Royal Engineers) tank at Courseulles was one of the 'funnies', tanks of the 79th Armoured Division. The AVRE fired a 40 lb (over 18 kg) 'petard' mine, which the soldiers called 'flying dustbins', to blow up pill-boxes and concrete gun positions.

Mulberry harbour

The **Allied** commanders had assumed, rightly, that they would not be able to capture a harbour big enough quickly. It needed to be large enough to land all the troops and supplies that would be necessary if the invasion was to be successful. From the beginning of the planning for an invasion they decided to build their own harbours, one at Omaha beach and one at Gold beach. It was essential that the Allied armies had a lot more supplies than the German defenders and that there should never be any shortages. Therefore it was vital to have safe, usable harbours from the beginning of the D-Day landings. The biggest of these was built at the town of Arromanches at the end of Gold beach and was given the codename 'Mulberry'. When it was completed it was called 'Port Winston' after the prime minister of Britain, Winston Churchill.

The basic idea was quite simple. About sixty old ships were to be sunk in lines to become **breakwaters** and reduce the waves. These were codenamed 'Gooseberry'. Also, 147 floating concrete blocks called 'Phoenix' were sunk to create areas sheltered from waves. Very big ships had to unload on the **seaward** side of the barrier. They were protected by floating 'bombardons' which reduced the height of waves. Inside the breakwater floating platforms were set up to unload ships. These stood on steel legs 30 metres high based on the seabed. The platforms moved up and down with the tide so that unloading need never be interrupted. Lastly, between 10 and 15 kilometres of flexible roadways resting on steel supports allowed the supplies to be brought ashore. All the parts of the Mulberry harbour were made in Britain and were towed across to Normandy by the Royal Navy from 7 June.

In August 1944, the Mulberry harbour at Arromanches was in full operation. There were no landings at Arromanches on D-Day as it was important that there should be no wreckage to delay the building of the artificial port.

While the artificial ports did not land as many supplies and troops as planned, they did a good job. Then, on 19 June, disaster struck as a three-day storm hit the harbours. Much of the equipment was wrecked and the cut back in supplies delayed some military action such as the advance on Cherbourg. The storm caused the abandonment of the Mulberry harbour at Omaha beach.

At low tide, this is what one of the concrete caissons at Arromanches looks like. The building of the Mulberry harbours was an enormous achievement.

The **engineers** fought back and repaired much of the damage and by the end of June 850,000 men, 150,000 vehicles and 600,000 tons of supplies had been landed in Normandy. By 26 July, ships were unloading at Cherbourg, which had now been captured. Petrol came ashore at Port-en-Bessin via PLUTO – a pipeline under the ocean, which pumped fuel from England to France. As other ports were captured, Mulberry was no longer needed and was closed on 19 November 1944.

Engineers played a vital part on D-Day, especially in the building of the artificial harbours. This is a memorial to the US 1st Special Engineers at Utah beach.

The wreckage of the Mulberry harbour at Arromanches still forms a huge semi-circle in the bay. The concrete caissons have resisted the pounding of storms and the waves for over 50 years. Detailed, working models of the Mulberry harbour can be seen in the D-Day museum in Arromanches.

The Battle of Normandy

After the D-Day landing beaches had been captured and the **Allied** troops started to move inland they began to face difficulties. The German troops had recovered from the shock of the landings and had been able to call up **reinforcements**. The main power of the Germans was concentrated on the city of Caen. The British and Canadian armies slogged away in a number of attacks that all failed to make much progress because the German **counter-attacks**, were deadly.

The Allies had intended to capture Caen on D-Day but this proved impossible. They tried to drive the Germans out by heavy bombing. The city was destroyed and its inhabitants suffered greatly. Field Marshal Rommel wanted to lead the German armies in a **retreat** to the River Seine but **Hitler** would not allow it. Hitler ordered his armies to fight and counter-attack. While they were inflicting heavy **casualties** on the Allies they were also being gradually worn down themselves.

Caen is the capital of Normandy and a large, bustling city. The skyline is dominated by the tall spire of the Saint-Pierre church.

Caen was largely destroyed in the fighting after D-Day. Heavy Allied bombing wrecked most buildings but failed to dislodge the German defenders.

This is the countryside of Normandy called 'bocage'. The sunken roads and high earth banks meant that Allied tanks could not be used properly and that German forces could launch surprise ambushes. Allied losses were high.

The Allied Tactical Air Force played a large part in the defeat of the German forces in Normandy. Ground attack fighters like this Hawker Typhoon with bombs and rockets, shown in the Memorial museum in Caen, were sent to attack the German troops wherever they found them.

The American army was able to move faster. They captured Cherbourg, a vital port for the Allies. After vicious fighting in their own '**battle of the hedgerows**' they captured the town of Saint Lo. General Bradley launched '**Cobra**' to break out of Normandy. Using **carpet bombing** and '**Rhinos**' (tanks) to cut through hedgerows, the US army pushed south to Avranches and then turned east in the final phase of the battle of Normandy. The British had captured most of Caen by 10th July and continued south. Hitler insisted that his troops attack the Americans at Mortain. It was a failure and the whole German army was in danger of being surrounded near the town of Falaise. The **Falaise pocket** was not closed quickly enough to prevent the escape of about 20,000 German soldiers but the rest were trapped, of these, 10,000 were killed and between 40,000 and 50,000 were captured. Allied planes rained destruction on the fleeing Germans. Those who could surrender did. The Battle of Normandy was at an end on 20 August 1944, 75 days after the D-Day landings.

The French people

France had surrendered in 1940. The German government decided that they would rule the northern half of France directly. A French government under Marshal Petain ruled the other part, which extended south of the River Loire. It agreed to co-operate with the Germans. It was called 'Vichy' France because the government was centred in the town called Vichy. Most French people hated the German occupation. Some secretly fought against the Germans. This was called the '**French Resistance**'. Any opposition was punished severely. Resistance fighters who were caught were executed or **deported** to **concentration camps**. **Hostages** were shot in places where Resistance fighters were caught as a punishment. Despite this, resistance continued and played a very important part in the D-Day landings. They provided much information about German defences.

In the tiny coastal hamlet of Le Home, this memorial remembers Bernard Anquetil, a Resistance fighter who was shot by the Germans in 1941, aged 24.

The commemoration of the 'Guyenne' and 'Tunisie' bomber squadrons is at the port of Grandcamp-Maisy. The French aircrews escaped to Britain and joined the RAF. They flew 'heavy' bombers during the invasion. The memorial says that one in two did not return.

The Free French Forces who fought with the Allies were led by General Charles de Gaulle. This street name displays a message that he sent to the people of occupied France promising to fight on until France was free again. 'Vive la France!' – 'Long Live France!'

During the night of 1 June the BBC sent a coded message. It was the first part of a sentence by the French poet Verlaine – 'The long sobs of the violins of autumn …' On 5 June they completed the sentence – '… wound my heart with languid monotony.' This was the signal that the landings would happen in the next two days. The Resistance blew up railway lines and bridges. They cut telephone wires. They did all they could to disrupt communications and prevent **reinforcements** reaching the landing beaches. The Germans retaliated by executing or deporting all the Resistance prisoners that they held in jail in Caen.

French people who escaped from occupied France formed the Free French Forces (FFF) which fought with the Allied forces. On D–Day a French and British **commando** group liberated the town of Ouistreham, and the warships *Georges-Leygues* and *Montcalm* bombarded the German defences, helping to put the fearsome Longues **battery** out of action finally.

The cost to the French people was great. As the **Allies** fought through the countryside, civilians were caught up in the fighting. Lives were lost and property was destroyed. Yet the French people celebrated because this was their liberation. This liberation is still commemorated today.

The Free French Sherman tank 'Berry au Bac' has been preserved at Arromanches to celebrate the part played by French soldiers in the liberation.

The 50th anniversary of the D-Day landings was a great celebration in Normandy. The gratitude of the French people to those who liberated them remains very strong.

WELCOME
BIENVENUE
1944 - 1994
Jubilé de la liberté en Normandie

Remembrance

The D-Day landings were paid for with the lives of men, most of them young. Thousands and thousands were killed or wounded. On D-Day itself the **Allies** landed 132,715 troops from the sea and 22,000 from the air. Of these, 9000 were wounded and 1000 were missing, some of whom turned up later. About 2000 were killed. Thus, despite the difficulties on Omaha beach the **casualties** for the landing were much lighter than the generals had feared. In the Battle for Normandy the losses grew much greater. By 21 August 1944, the Allies had 209,672 casualties, 36,976 of these had been killed. In addition, about 28,000 airmen had been killed in the preparations for, and during, the landings. Many of those who died have no known graves as their bodies were never found or could not be identified. Others are buried in beautifully kept cemeteries that are scattered across the region of the battle.

Not all the Allied losses were from the USA, Britain and Canada. Soldiers, sailors, airmen, civilians and merchant seamen of many nations lost their lives in the fight for freedom against the **Nazis**.

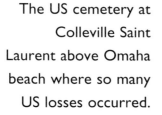

The US cemetery at Colleville Saint Laurent above Omaha beach where so many US losses occurred.

The largest British cemetery is at Bayeux. It contains the graves of many British servicemen. Men from Germany, Poland and some other countries are buried there as well.

Some of the bodies of American servicemen were taken back to the USA at the request of their families. Others lie in two cemeteries, Saint James near Brittany and Colleville Saint Laurent at the top of the cliff above Omaha Beach. In Colleville there are nearly 10,000 graves in an area, now peaceful and beautiful, that was, on D-Day, the scene of bitter fighting.

It is the tradition of the British forces that its dead are buried where they fell in action. Thus there are a number of British and Canadian cemeteries throughout the region of fighting. Additionally, French villagers often buried airmen and small groups of soldiers in their parish churchyards. Here they remain, tended by the local community.

The bodies of some who died were never found. Others could not be identified. In British and Commonwealth cemeteries their graves are marked as 'Known unto God'.

25

Memorials

The sacrifice was made on all sides. Nobody really knows how many of the German army were killed in the Normandy campaign. They were mostly ordinary people but they were in the grip of an evil leader. There are about 75,000 graves in German war cemeteries. What is certain is that the enemies who fought so bitterly in Normandy in 1944 are now friends and allies. As well as recognizing the heroism and sacrifice of the past, the overwhelming theme of Normandy today is remembrance and peace.

There are permanent memorials to the groups who took part in the D-Day landings, such as regiments and armies. There are also memorials to individuals. Sometimes these are commemorated in something as simple as a road name, often to remember a brave man who gave his life in a particular place in the cause of freedom.

This grave belongs to a German soldier killed on D-Day.

Eyewitness

This is an adaptation of the memories of Elsie Guilbert who lived in East London and was 16 years old in 1944: 'The soldier I met was called Harry. He was in the East Lancashire Regiment with four friends. He asked me to go for a walk with him. I wrote my name and address for him. We were both very shy so we never exchanged a kiss. Then, suddenly, they were gone. Harry wrote to me later saying that his friends Vic and Tony had been killed in the landings and then Oliver and Jack had been killed in Normandy. We wrote to each other for many months and then his letters stopped. There is no official record of him being killed in the war so I hope he is alive and happy somewhere.'

We Remember D-Day, Frank and Joan Shaw

The main German cemetery is at La Cambe. The dead are remembered by named plaques, groups of five crosses and a central memorial.

There are many memorials to the great events of D-Day 6 June 1944 and the following months until France was liberated. Clockwise from top: a road sign commemorating Major Howard, who led the capture of Pegasus bridge, at Bénouville; a square at Arromanches is named after General Leclerc's Free French **armoured** division; a road has been named to honour a US **engineer** killed at Utah beach; a memorial to the US 90th division at Utah beach; the memorial to the 'Big Red One' – the First Infantry Division of the US Army, on the heights above Omaha beach; a 'signal-memorial'. These were built, all along the invasion coast, by the French government after the war to commemorate the liberation of 6 June 1944.

Timeline

1939	3 September: Britain and France declare war on **Nazi** Germany after the German invasion of Poland
1940	17 June: France surrenders to Germany
1941	22 June: Germany attacks USSR, and USSR asks USA and UK for help by fighting against Germany in Western Europe
1943	January: Churchill and Roosevelt agree to prepare a plan to land in Europe
	24 December: General Eisenhower named as Supreme **Allied** Commander in Chief of Allied Forces to carry out the landings, codenamed 'Overlord'
1944	March: Allied bombing campaign began destroying German defences and communications
	6 June: D-Day landings in Normandy by Allied forces
	13 June: British advance stopped by German tanks at Villers-Bocage
	27 June: US army takes Cherbourg
	7 July: German **counter-attack** at Mortain defeated
	9 July: British army begins its final capture of Caen
	17 August: Falaise captured. German army surrounded.
	20 August: Eisenhower says battle of Normandy is over
	25 August: Paris liberated by Allies
1945	30 April: **Hitler** kills himself
	8 May: Germany surrenders to the Allies. The Second World War in Europe is over.

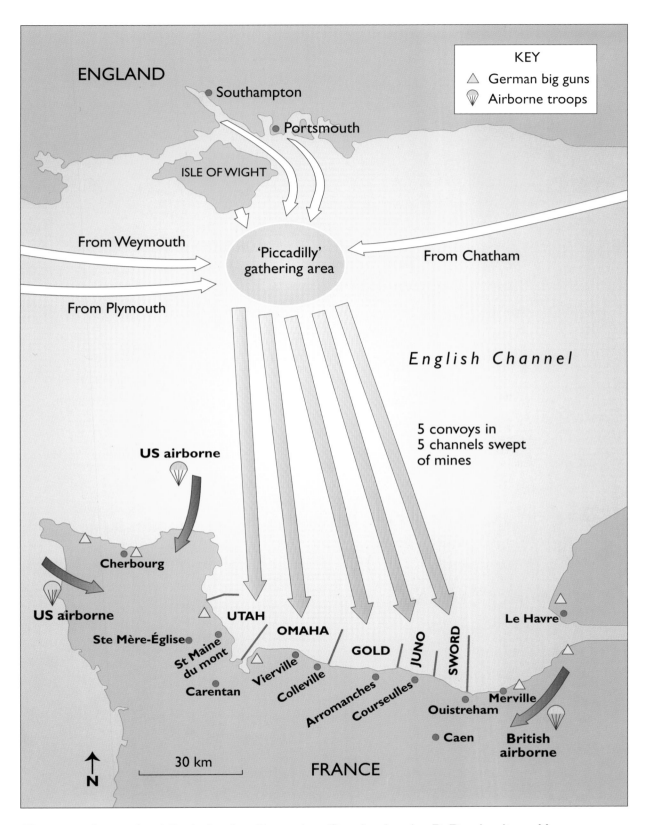

KEY
△ German big guns
⛱ Airborne troops

ENGLAND

Southampton

Portsmouth

ISLE OF WIGHT

From Weymouth

'Piccadilly' gathering area

From Chatham

From Plymouth

English Channel

5 convoys in
5 channels swept
of mines

US airborne

Cherbourg

US airborne

Le Havre

Ste Mère-Église

UTAH

OMAHA

GOLD

JUNO

SWORD

St Maine du mont

Vierville

Colleville

Arromanches

Courseulles

Merville

Carentan

Ouistreham

British airborne

Caen

30 km

N

FRANCE

This map shows the Allied plan for Operation Overlord – the D-Day landings. You can use this map to support the information in each section to see where the events happened.

29

Glossary

Allies countries that joined together to fight Germany, Italy and Japan in the Second World War. The main ones were USA, Free France, UK and its Empire and the USSR.

armour vehicles like tanks were protected by thick plates of metal called armour

artillery big guns that fired explosive shells rather than bullets

assault troops soldiers who are the first to land or who lead the attack

automatic gunfire fast streams of bullets (fire) from machine guns

AVRE Armoured Vehicle Royal Engineers. These were specially adapted tanks to help capture the beaches.

barbed wire twisted wire with spikes or blades in it to stop soldiers moving past it

battery group of big guns

Battle of the Atlantic battle from 1940 to 1944 between German submarines and Allied warships to protect convoys of supplies from the USA to the UK

battle of the hedgerows fierce fighting in the fields of Normandy

battleships huge warships with big guns

bombardment firing lots of artillery shells at the same target

breakwater obstacle, like a sunken ship, that breaks up the waves coming ashore

bridgehead land occupied by the Allied armies after the landings

carpet bombing dropping bombs accurately and closely together in front of advancing troops to destroy the enemy

casualties troops who are killed or wounded

Cobra codename for the American breakout from the bridgehead

commandos group of soldiers trained to carry out special missions

command posts places where military leaders send orders to their soldiers

concentration camps prison camps where opponents and victims of the Nazis were sent, often to be killed

counter-attack an attack by defenders to hit back at the first attackers

deport take people away from their home or country to Nazi concentration camps

engineer soldier who is trained to build roads and bridges and also to deal with explosives and obstacles

Falaise pocket area of land east of the town of Falaise where most of the German army was trapped in August 1944

French Resistance French people who fought against the German occupation

frogmen underwater swimmers using breathing devices

garrison group of soldiers based in a town or village

glider aircraft with no engine. They are towed into the air and to their destination by powered aeroplanes.

gun emplacements places where big guns were located

Hitler Adolf Hitler (1884–1945) leader of Germany 1933–45

hostage innocent person held under threat of punishment to ensure obedience by others

landing craft boat specially designed to put men and equipment on shore

Luftwaffe German airforce

mines explosive devices which go off when touched or trodden on

mortars kind of gun that fires bombs high in the air to rain down on an enemy

Nazi someone or something that followed the ideas of the German political group led by Hitler, the National Socialist German Workers' Party

pill-boxes defensive concrete buildings housing machine guns

planned objectives ideas or places that leaders want to achieve or reach

play dead pretend to be dead

reinforced concrete bunkers buildings for shelter. The concrete used to make them was strengthened with metal rods.

reinforcements extra troops brought to help the originals

retreat move back or away from fighting

Rhinos US Sherman tanks with sharp bulldozer blades to cut through earth banks

seaward side near the sea rather than the land

signaler soldier or sailor who sends messages

strong-point area where defensive bunkers and guns are concentrated

strafe shoot at the ground from an aircraft

U-boat German submarine

Index

Titles in the *Visiting the past* series include:

Hardback   0 431 02786 2

Hardback   0 431 02787 0

Hardback   0 431 02784 6

Hardback   0 431 02785 4

Find out about the other titles in this series on our website www.heinemann.co.uk/library